MW00954631

HOW TO DRAW BASKETBALL PLAYERS FOR KIDS

Copyright © 2019 Tony R. Smith All Rights Reserved.

No part of this publication may be reproduced, distributed, or transmitted in any form or by any means, including photocopying, recording, or other electronic or mechanical methods, or by any information storage and retrieval system without the prior written permission of Smith Show Publishing, except in the case of very brief quotations embodied in critical reviews and certain other noncommercial uses permitted by copyright law.

Example #1 Practice

Example of (Smudge Shading). Smudge Shading will give your drawing a complete look.

Example of (Tonal Shading). Tonal Shading will give your drawing a smooth contrast finish.

Example of (Hatching Shading). Hatching Shading will help blend your drawing together.

Example of (Light Smudge Shading). Light Smudge Shading will give your drawing a complete look.

Example #1 Final

STAGE 1

STAGE 2

FINAL STAGE

DRAW/SKETCH

DRAW/SKETCH

DRAW/SKETCH

DRAW/SKETCH

DRAW/SKETCH

DRAW/SKETCH

DRAW/SKETCH

DRAW/SKETCH

DRAW/SKETCH

DRAW/SKETCH

DRAW/SKETCH

DRAW/SKETCH

DRAW/SKETCH

DRAW/SKETCH

DRAW/SKETCH

DRAW/SKETCH

DRAW/SKETCH

DRAW/SKETCH

DRAW/SKETCH

DRAW/SKETCH

DRAW/SKETCH

DRAW/SKETCH

DRAW/SKETCH

DRAW/SKETCH

DRAW/SKETCH

DRAW/SKETCH

DRAW/SKETCH

DRAW/SKETCH

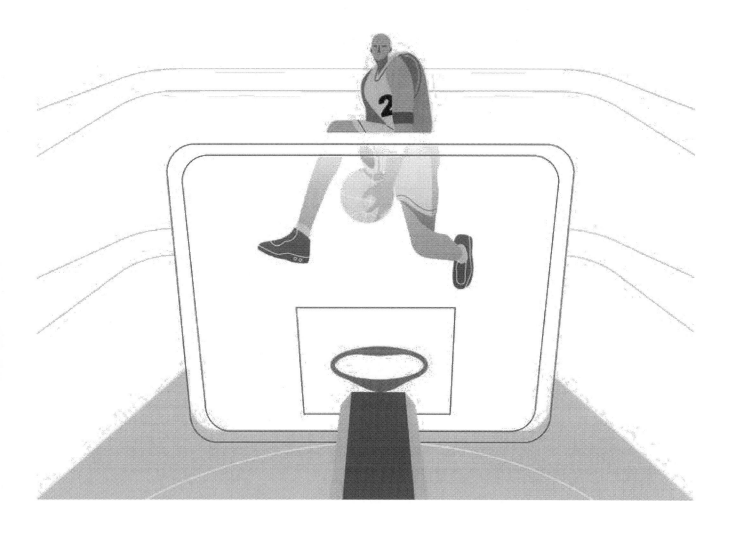

DRAW/SKETCH

DRAW/SKETCH

DRAW/SKETCH

DRAW/SKETCH

DRAW/SKETCH

DRAW/SKETCH

DRAW/SKETCH

DRAW/SKETCH

DRAW/SKETCH

DRAW/SKETCH

DRAW/SKETCH

DRAW/SKETCH

DRAW/SKETCH

DRAW/SKETCH

DRAW/SKETCH

DRAW/SKETCH

DRAW/SKETCH

DRAW/SKETCH

DRAW/SKETCH

DRAW/SKETCH

DRAW/SKETCH

BASKETBALL
S P O R T B A C K G R O U N D

DRAW/SKETCH

DRAW/SKETCH

DRAW/SKETCH

DRAW/SKETCH

DRAW/SKETCH

DRAW/SKETCH

DRAW/SKETCH

DRAW/SKETCH

DRAW/SKETCH

Made in the USA
Columbia, SC
21 December 2020

29346302R00063